First World War
and Army of Occupation
War Diary
France, Belgium and Germany

48 DIVISION
Divisional Troops
Divisional Trench Mortar Batteries
21 April 1916 - 30 October 1917

WO95/2750/3

The Naval & Military Press Ltd
www.nmarchive.com
Published in association with The National Archives

Published by

The Naval & Military Press Ltd

Unit 10 Ridgewood Industrial Park,

Uckfield, East Sussex,

TN22 5QE England

Tel: +44 (0) 1825 749494

www.naval-military-press.com

www.nmarchive.com

This diary has been reprinted in facsimile from the original. Any imperfections are inevitably reproduced and the quality may fall short of modern type and cartographic standards.

© **Crown Copyright**
Images reproduced by permission of The National Archives, London, England, 2015.

Contents

Document type	Place/Title	Date From	Date To
Heading	WO95/2750/3		
Heading	48th Division BEF 48th Divl Trench Mortar Btts Apr 1916-Oct 1917		
Heading	War Diary Of 48th Divl Artillery Trench Mortar Batteries From April 1916 To August 1916 (Volume I)		
War Diary	Valheureux	21/04/1916	28/04/1916
War Diary	Hebuterne	29/04/1916	19/07/1916
War Diary	Coineaux	20/07/1916	21/07/1916
War Diary	Aveluy	22/07/1916	30/08/1916
War Diary	Hebuterne	20/05/1916	20/07/1916
War Diary	Coineaux	20/07/1916	20/07/1916
War Diary	Aveluy	21/07/1916	30/08/1916
Heading	48th Divisional Artillery 48th Trench Mortar Battery September 1916		
War Diary	Aveluy	01/09/1916	30/09/1916
Heading	War Diary Of 48th Divl Artillery Trench Mortar Batteries October 1916 Volume Part II		
War Diary	In The Field	03/10/1916	31/10/1916
Heading	War Diary Of 48th Divisional Artillery Trench Mortar Battys November 1916 Volume Part III		
War Diary	Hebuterne	01/11/1916	20/11/1916
War Diary	Fonquevillers	21/11/1916	24/11/1916
War Diary	Souastre	26/11/1916	26/11/1916
War Diary	Barly	30/11/1916	30/11/1916
Heading	War Diary of 48th Divse. Artillery Trench Mortar Batteries December 1916 (Volume Part I)		
War Diary	Talmas	01/12/1916	01/12/1916
War Diary	Frechencourt	02/12/1916	07/12/1916
War Diary	Contalmaison	08/12/1916	31/12/1916
Heading	War Diary Of 48th Divisional Artillery Trench Mortar Batteries January 1917 Volume III Part II		
War Diary	In The Field	16/01/1917	26/01/1917
Heading	War Diary Of 48th Divisional Artillery Trench Mortar Batteries February 1917 Volume III Part III		
War Diary	Cappy	02/02/1917	28/02/1917
Heading	War Diary Of 48th Divisional Artillery Trench Mortar Batteries March 1917 Volume IV Part I		
War Diary	Biaches Barleux Line	01/03/1917	31/03/1917
Heading	War Diary Of 48th Div Arty Trench Mortar Batteries April 1917 Volume 4 Part 2		
War Diary	In The Field	01/04/1917	29/04/1917
Heading	War Diary Of 48th Divisional Artillery Trench Mortar Batteries May 1917 Volume IV Part II		
War Diary	Peronne	01/05/1917	07/05/1917
War Diary	Fremont	08/05/1917	16/05/1917
War Diary	Le Transloy	17/05/1917	18/05/1917
War Diary	Beaumetz Les Cambrai	20/05/1917	31/05/1917
Heading	War Diary Of 48th Divisional Artillery Trench Mortar Batteries June 1917 Volume V Part 1		
War Diary	Beaumetz Les Cambrai	01/06/1917	22/06/1917

War Diary	Beugny	23/06/1917	23/06/1917
War Diary	Mametz	24/06/1917	26/07/1917
Heading	War Diary Of 48th Divisional Artillery Trench Mortar Batteries July 1917 Volume 5 Part 2		
War Diary		27/07/1917	29/07/1917
War Diary	Vlamertinghe	01/08/1917	31/08/1917
Heading	48th Trench Mortar Batteries RA War Diary August 1917 Volume V Part III		
War Diary	In The Field	01/09/1917	30/09/1917
Heading	48th Trench Mortar Batteries R.A. War Diary September 1917 Volume VI Part I		
War Diary	In The Field	01/10/1917	30/10/1917
Heading	War Diary Of 48th Trench Mortar Batteries R.A October 1917 Volume VI Part II		

W9a5|2750|3

48TH DIVISION

BEF

48TH DIVL. TRENCH MORTAR BTTS.

APR 1916 - ~~MAR 1919~~

Oct 1917

TO ITALY

48TH DIVISION

VOL I

Confidential

War Diary
of
48th Divl. Artillery, Trench Mortar Batteries.

from April 1916 to August 1916

(Volume I)

Vol 19

R H Millan, Captain
D.T.M.O., 48th. Divn.

F.

48th Division

V.48. Trench Mortar Batt
(Heavy Mortar)

Army Form C. 2118

WAR DIARY
or
INTELLIGENCE SUMMARY
(Erase heading not required.)

Instructions regarding War Diaries and Intelligence Summaries are contained in F.S. Regs., Part II. and the Staff Manual respectively. Title Pages will be prepared in manuscript.

Place	Date	Hour	Summary of Events and Information	Remarks and references to Appendices
	1916 APRIL			
VALHEUREUX	21		Battery Formed. Details of Battery assembled at Army School of Mortars for training.	
	28		Battery left School and went into Lines at HEBUTERNE	
HEBUTERNE	29 to JUNE 24		Battery personnel employed in preparation of Gun pits.	
	25		Commenced Mounting Gun. Railway Bombardment Commenced.	
	26		Commencement of Preliminary Bombardment. Battery not in action.	
	27		"W" Day of Bombardment. Gun in Action. Objective given as Front Line trenches from HOOK towards front of SERRE.	
	28		Battery in Action throughout Bombardment. Fired approx 30 rounds daily on above objectives. Every Scored direct hits on edge of Gun pit repeatedly and without pulling gun out of action. Repairs carried out during nights.	
	29			
	30			
	JULY 1		Day of assault. Batt in action throughout. No unit above a form in 615 y/Shell.	
	2 to 13		Repairing Gun pits and completing Ammunition dugouts. Quiet on Front.	
	14		Battery in Action. Objectives as above. Enemy replied with Lacrymatory Shell.	
	15		" " " " " " Finally Gun detachment temporarily out of action.	

48th Division.

V48 Trench Mortar Battery
or
Heavy Mortar 9.45

Army Form C. 2118

WAR DIARY
or
INTELLIGENCE SUMMARY
(Erase heading not required.)

Place	Date	Hour	Summary of Events and Information	Remarks and references to Appendices
HEBUTERNE	JULY 16 to 19		Quiet on front. Battery personnel refacing gun pits.	
	20		R.F.A details left to COIGNEAUX. leaving R.G.A. details at HEBUTERNE attached to 38th DIV.	
COIGNEAUX	21		Battery left to join Guns at OVILLERS. arrived at AVELUY	
AVELUY	22		Took over Guns from 12th DIV.	
	23		Preparing gun pits.	
	24 to 28		Batt in action. objectives German Strong points at go.	
			Batt in action each day.	
	29 to AUG. 9		Moved out to ST. OUEN after handing over to 12th DIV. { at ST. OUEN at rest.	
	10		Moved out to ORVILLE en route to AVELUY	
	13		Arrived at AVELUY and took over from 12th DIV.	
	14		Batt in action at OVILLERS. Considerable damage done to Enemy Strong points in neighbourhood of Point 25-09.14.	

WAR DIARY
or
INTELLIGENCE SUMMARY

(Erase heading not required.)

Army Form C. 2118

V. 48th Then el Motor Battery
Heavy M.G. Bn. 9/45

III. 48th Division.

Place	Date	Hour	Summary of Events and Information	Remarks and references to Appendices
AVELUY	AUG. 15 to 28		Battery in action. Each day objectives every 3 hours/point in X.32. Menaced our guns in AUTHUILLE WOOD and engaged show points in vicinity/-Point 56. Heavy enemy barrage on WOOD on 21st caused 9 casualties, gun undamaged. Our gun removed from near OVILLERS CHURCH 15th in forward position. New gun put in command at point 90. During above [B.O. Battery] co-operated in bombardment preliminary to infantry attacks.	
	29		Relieved by 25th Division who took over all guns and shot. Batteries remained temporarily at AVELUY & Buttery. 17cm Minenwerfer at point 44. - The gun appears to be in comfort with some 16 rounds comfort. a	
	30		Battery in Billets at AVELUY. Weather broke by bad heavy rain.	

30/9/16

R.W. Mellor Capt.
D.T.M.O.

48th Division

Auklur Flend Mular Batteries

Batteries "X - Y - Z"

Army Form C. 2118

WAR DIARY
or
INTELLIGENCE SUMMARY
(Erase heading not required.)

Instructions regarding War Diaries and Intelligence Summaries are contained in F.S. Regs., Part II. and the Staff Manual respectively. Title Pages will be prepared in manuscript.

Place	Date	Hour	Summary of Events and Information	Remarks and references to Appendices
HEBUTERNE	1916 MAY 20 to JUNE 10		Battries in line at HEBUTERNE alternated on battery been held at COUIN in turn. The available period of TMs on the half have inflicted from troops and during this period two (2) bombardments of wire carried out. Enemy retaliation was so heavy in one case as to completely destroy gun pits. No new bombardment carried out during June made of infantry 20 rounds been fired in every [?] line trenches.	
	11 to 23		X, Y + Z Batteries in line at HEBUTERNE (and in preparations built emplacements. Gun at in action moderate shell in front during this period. Same interrupting progress of work.	
	24		Commencement of Preliminary Bombardment "U Day"	
	25		"V" Day. Heavy Bombardment (Enemy front positions by Div. Arty)	
	26 to JULY 1		W Day. Batteries in action during period of silence bombardments. Repulses. Enemy wire an total of 1/4 line trenches. Bombardment continued as above each day. Average of 50 rnds per gun fixed. Sir pits heavy retaliated to each day at 77m/m +15 cm shells + gun pits considerably damaged each day but refused during night + firing at unchanged next day. 3 guns out however remained in action in day of assault — remainder of batteries damaged beyond repair during bombardment casualties were	

II 48th Division Medium Trench Mortar Batteries
Batteries X. Y – Z

WAR DIARY
or
INTELLIGENCE SUMMARY

Army Form C. 2118

(Erase heading not required.)

Instructions regarding War Diaries and Intelligence Summaries are contained in F.S. Regs., Part II. and the Staff Manual respectively. Title Pages will be prepared in manuscript.

Place	Date	Hour	Summary of Events and Information	Remarks and references to Appendices
HEBUTERNE	JULY 1		Note Slight. One man and crew killed in action. Several casualties being received in Bullets from Sere Par.	
	to		Day of assault on SERRE.	
	2 to 4		Batteries. Infantry. Scenes of gun fire HEBUTERNE. Received shelled at intervals each day.	
	5		X & 2 Batteries out to COUIN Street.	
	6		One Batty Z 23 from 16 COUIN Street.	
	7		2.23 Batt came in COUIN - X Batt Infantry gun pits HEBUTERNE. Considerable truck in front.	
	8		X Batty Infantry gun pits at HEBUTERNE. Quiet day in front.	
	9		" "	
			2/Lieut Evers joined. 2 Batt. came took over command. Vice Lt Palmer Sick.	
	13		Quiet in front. Batteries X & Y Infantry gun pits at HEBUTERNE.	
	14		"2" Batt Moved to COLLINCAMPS.	
	15 to 20		2 Batt 48th & 2.23 Batt Commenced making gun pits in COLLINCAMPS Sector. X & Y Batts Infantry gun pits at HEBUTERNE	

1875 Wt. W593/826 1,000,000 4/15 J.B.C. & A. A.D.S.S./Forms/C. 2118.

48th Division
Medium Trench Mortar Batteries
Batteries X.Y.Z.

Army Form C. 2118

WAR DIARY
or
INTELLIGENCE SUMMARY
(Erase heading not required.)

Instructions regarding War Diaries and Intelligence Summaries are contained in F.S. Regs., Part II. and the Staff Manual respectively. Title Pages will be prepared in manuscript.

Place	Date	Hour	Summary of Events and Information	Remarks and references to Appendices
COINEAUX	JULY 20		Batteries moved out to COINEAUX	
AVELUY	21		Batteries left COINEAUX and arrived at AVELUY 1020 into lines at OVILLERS	
	22		Took over guns in the line from 12th Div.	
	24		Shd bombardment. Moderate shut in front	
	25 to 28		Carried out Shd bombardment. Enemy Shey bomb near point 90	
			Carried out Shd bombardment. Helm was intermittent and lt.	
	29		Moved out to ST OUEN les Herrings. Been relieved by 12th Division.	
AUG 9			In hested ST OUEN	
	10		Moved to ORVILLE	
	11			
	12		at ORVILLE	
	13		Arrived at AVELUY and took over guns in line from 12th Div. two batteries in the line 4/3 8 guns. Personnel remaining in action In depot 3 been relieved & personnel of other batteries every 3rd day	
	14		X Batt in action. Enjoyed Shey bomb 70 b. 44 + 55 m X 2 R.	

IV 48th Division. Medium Trench Mortar Battery
X - Y - Z

Army Form C. 2118

WAR DIARY
or
INTELLIGENCE SUMMARY
(Erase heading not required.)

Place	Date	Hour	Summary of Events and Information	Remarks and references to Appendices
AVELUY	AUG 15		X Batt. Engaged Enemy points 20 & 44 G.2.55 in X2c. Enemy ammunition points blown up.	
	16		X Batt. Engaged Enemy Strong points and obtained direct hits on Strong points 26 & 20	
	17		Y. Batt. engaged Strong points 39 & 62 with very successful results. Enemy everywhere brought down in "No man's Land". Our bombardment.	
	18			
	19			
	20		One gun 1- X Batt advanced 150 yds & at Eversight interaction	
	21		2 Batt mounted 3 guns in AUTHUILLE WOOD but Rear shelling of enemy levelled gun & my trouble uptoelw.	
	"		X Batt. carried out bombardment in every Strong points here other and 4pm but out of 4 o'clock centered, 1 or killed & 2 wounded.	
	22		Bombarded — enemy (X Batt) Enemy Strong points 79 - X2a cal. 25. 24.43 - R.32.c.	
			2. Batt Engaged points 98 & 58 in X1 wire cut, trench lines our objective.	

Z 48th DIVISION

WAR DIARY
Medium Trench Mortar Batteries
Batteries X - Y - Z

INTELLIGENCE SUMMARY
(Erase heading not required.)

Army Form C. 2118

Place	Date	Hour	Summary of Events and Information	Remarks and references to Appendices
AVELUY	AUG 23		No Bombardments carried out.	
	24		Y Batt engaged Point 44 - various enemy posns.	
	25		Y Batt registered on front 03 - R.32.d	
	26		Z Bombardment. Guns dealt with at work changing position / guns.	
	27		Z Batt. Carry out bombardment preliminary to infantry attack.	
	28		Z Batt Third of the Guns preparation to taken part in our assault. Various enemy bombardments relieved. No active enemy retaliation. Some bombardment & very heavy shelling from front line.	
	29		Relieved & 1st Division who took over. Guns & Howitzers (8 guns)	
	30		Batteries remain at AVELUY pending movement away.	

30/1/

R.H.Williams Capt.
D.T.M.B

48th. DIVISIONAL ARTILLERY

48th. TRENCH MORTAR BATTERY

SEPTEMBER 1916.

Army Form C. 2118.

WAR DIARY or **INTELLIGENCE SUMMARY**

48th Divisional Artillery — Heavy and Medium Trench Mortar Batts. Trench Mortar Batts. V, X, Y + Z. Batts.

(Erase heading not required.)

Place	Date	Hour	Summary of Events and Information	Remarks and references to Appendices
	1916			
AVELUY	Sept 1		Batteries out at rest — Fatigue parties working daily salving French mortar ammunition for OVILLERS trenches and clearing and renovating same at Headquarters.	
	6		5 - 2" T. Mortars taken over from 25th Div.	
"	11		At rest.	
"	12		Personnel employed on three mortars — rifle revolver practice a Range Fatigue parties making gun pits at MARTINSART	
	16			
"	17		Personnel employed at gun pits for 48th Div. R.A. relieve POZIERS and OVILLERS	
	18			
	19			
"	20 to 23		Ditto and finding fatigue parties for 11th Div. Withdrawing Heavy mortars from AUTHUILLE WOOD	
"	24		Fatigue parties working for D/243 Batt. RFA	
	25		" " "	
	26		V 48 Tm. Batt. Mounting Mortars for X 11 Batte.	
	27 to 30		Minor fatigues — mainly gun pits. infantry for moving out. Calcutta a THIEPVAL & 11th Div.	

G.H. Wilson Capt.
D.T.M.O

389/16

Original

Vol I

Confidential.

War Diary
of
48th Divl. Artillery Trench Mortar Batteries

October 1916.

Volume I. Part II

31/10/16.

A.R. Hopkins. Captain T.R.F.A.
D.T.M.O. 48th Division.

Army Form C. 2118.

WAR DIARY
or
INTELLIGENCE SUMMARY
(Erase heading not required.)

Place	Date	Hour	Summary of Events and Information	Remarks and references to Appendices
In the Field.	3.10.16		48th Trench Mortar Batteries moved from AVELUY to HEBUTERNE.	
	4.10.16		Two Heavy Mortars taken over from 33rd Division, one emplacement at FONQUEVILLERS, one at North end of HEBUTERNE.	
	7.10.16		Medium Batteries registering.	
	9.10.16		Enemy shelled village heavily for three hours during night, mostly gas shells. 1 casualty in Z Battery.	
	17.10.16		Three Heavy Mortars taken over from 17th, 33rd & 49th Divisions. The first two named in HEBUTERNE, the other in FONQUEVILLERS. Also four medium mortars from 17th Div and four from 33rd Div.	
	18.10.16 & 21.10.16		Medium Batteries wire-cutting in front of Enemy trenches T/T FIND FIRM F/G. Considerable damage done. Enemy retaliated heavily on each occasion causing 1 casualty in Y Battery	

Army Form C. 2118.

WAR DIARY
or
INTELLIGENCE SUMMARY
(Erase heading not required.)

Place	Date	Hour	Summary of Events and Information	Remarks and references to Appendices
	22.10.16		CAPT WIGLAN RFA handed over duties as D.T.M.O to CAPT HOPKINS RFA of V48 By.	
	24.10.16		Heavy Ammunition moved to TENQUEVILLERS in G.S. Wagons, to make up 30 rounds per gun.	
	26.10.16		Three Heavy Mortars in action. 33 rounds fired. Shooting erratic and unsatisfactory owing to faulty ammunition.	
	28.10.16		Medium mortars wire cutting in front of Enemy trench TOOLERY. 2 casualties in X Battery from enemy trench mortar fire.	
	29.10.16		One man X Battery wounded in HWK.	
	29.10.16 to 31.10.16		Work at a standstill owing to violent rain. Two casualties Z Battery. Enemy shell fire in HWKS.	

A.W. Hopkins
Capt RFA
D.T.M.O.

Original.

Vol 8

Confidential.

War Diary

of

48th Divisional Artillery Trench Mortar Battys

November 1916.

Volume ~~II~~   Part III

30/11/16.

A R Hopkins
D.T.M.O   Captain. T. R.F.A.
          48th Division

Army Form C. 2118.

WAR DIARY or INTELLIGENCE SUMMARY.

48th Trench Mortar Battery. D.T.M.O. 48th Division. 30/11/16

(Erase heading not required.)

Instructions regarding War Diaries and Intelligence Summaries are contained in F. S. Regs., Part II. and the Staff Manual respectively. Title pages will be prepared in manuscript.

Place	Date	Hour	Summary of Events and Information	Remarks and references to Appendices
HEBUTERNE	November 1st to 10th		Medium Batteries working on emplacement & carrying out normal retaliatory firing, usually in reply to enemy minenwerfer, & upset of Infantry.	
	13th		Special Operation with R.E. Smoke Bombs. 3 medium Batteries in action. Smoke Barrage followed by wirecutting.	
	14th to 20th		Medium Batteries wirecutting.	
FONQUEVILLERS	21st		Personnel moved from HEBUTERNE to FONQUEVILLERS, on relief of Divisional Front. 3 Heavy mortars in HEBUTERNE handed over to 31st Division.	
	23rd		Heavy Battery commenced work on new railway inside lisière line at FONQUEVILLERS. The new railway mounting for 9.45" mortar	

Army Form C. 2118.

WAR DIARY
or
INTELLIGENCE SUMMARY.

(Erase heading not required.)

Instructions regarding War Diaries and Intelligence Summaries are contained in F. S. Regs., Part II. and the Staff Manual respectively. Title pages will be prepared in manuscript.

Place	Date	Hour	Summary of Events and Information	Remarks and references to Appendices
	24th		2 Battery engaged enemy wire opposite MONCHY, to cut gaps for Infantry. This was done with success. Weather very bad at the time.	
SOUASTRE	26th		Personnel of all Batteries moved out to SOUASTRE. Four Heavy Mortars handed over to 49th Division – Two being in action in front of FONQUEVILLERS, and two on the Dump at HENU. All 9.45" & 2 inch ammunition in charge handed over.	
BARLY	30th		Personnel of all Batteries moved from SOUASTRE to BARLY.	

A. Stephens Capt. RFA.
D.T.M.O. 48th Division

Original

Confidential.

War Diary

of

48th Divs. Artillery Trench Mortar Batteries

December 1916.

(Volume ~~III~~ Part I)

Captain.
D.T.M.O. 48th Division.

WAR DIARY or INTELLIGENCE SUMMARY

Army Form C. 2118.

D.T.M.O. 48th T.M. Batteries.

December 1916.

Place	Date	Hour	Summary of Events and Information	Remarks and references to Appendices
TALMAS	1.		All batteries billeted for one night.	
FRECHENCOURT	2. 6/7		Arrived FRECHENCOURT. Billetted with D.A.C. Command. Rifle drill & various working parties supplied. Inspection by Col Browne comdg 48 D.A.C. on 4th inst.	
CONTALMAISON	8		Moved to PEAKE WOOD, CONTALMAISON in motor lorries. Billeted in bivouacs.	
	9.		Moved into dugouts, owing to bivouacs being heavily shelled on night 8/9.	
	10 to 31		Supplied working parties for constructing Telephone Exchange at VILLA WOOD, Erecting huts & stabling for 48 D.A. Also billeting roads at B Echelon 48 D.A.C. Two officers sent to 240 Bde for attachment. One to Divnl School for Infantry Course. One to T.M. School for Course.	

B. Hopkins Capt. D.T.M.O.

Original. Confidential.

War Diary

of

48th Divisional Artillery Trench Mortar Batteries

January. 1917.

Volume III. Part II

Duncan MacIver
CAPT,
D.T.M.O. 48 DIV.

D.T.M.O.

WAR DIARY
or
INTELLIGENCE SUMMARY
(Erase heading not required.)

Army Form C. 2118.

48th Div. Only.
Trench Mortar Batteries
January. 1917.

Place	Date	Hour	Summary of Events and Information	Remarks and references to Appendices
In the field	16.1.17	—	Trench Mortar Batteries moved to FRECHENCOURT	
	19.1.17 / 29.1.17		X48. Trench Mortar Battery went to School of Mortars 4. Army.	
"	26.1.17	—	Trench Mortar Batteries moved to HAMELET	

Duncan MacThrogen
Capt.
D.T.M.O. 48 Div.

Original.

Vol XI

Confidential.

War Diary.

of

48th Divisional Artillery Trench Mortar Batteries.

February 1917.

Volume III. Part III.

.... Capt.
D.T.M.O. 48 Div.

Army Form C. 2118.

48 TRENCH MORTAR BATTERIES. WAR DIARY or INTELLIGENCE SUMMARY

(Erase heading not required.)

February 1917.

Place	Date	Hour	Summary of Events and Information	Remarks and references to Appendices
CAPPY	2.2.17 to 28.2.17		48 T.M. Batteries quartered at the A.R.P. on CAPPY - HERBÉCOURT Road. D.T.M.O's Head Qrs situated at HERBÉCOURT CEMETERY.	
	2.2.17 to 18.2.17		Batteries working on emplacements. Work almost impossible owing to intense frost & hardness of ground.	
	19.2.17		248 Battery wire cutting.	
	20.2.17 to 24.2.17		All work impossible owing to thaw & general collapse of trenches which are impassable, almost everywhere waist deep in mud.	
	20.2.17 to 21.2.17		Extra Batteries arrived to reinforce, X 50, Y 50, 21.	
	25.2.17 to 28.2.17		Work resumed, all communications being enjoined to works over the top. All trenches impassable.	

Matthews Capt.
D.T.M.O.

Confidential.   Original.

War Diary

of

48th Divisional Artillery Trench Mortar Batteries

March 1917.

Volume IV. Part 1.

48 TRENCH MORTAR BATTERIES. R.A. WAR DIARY or INTELLIGENCE SUMMARY.

Army Form C. 2118.

Place	Date	Hour	Summary of Events and Information	Remarks and references to Appendices
BIACHES - BARLEUX LINE	March 1st to 5th		Batteries working on completion of emplacements & filling up ammunition.	
	6th to 12th		Heavy Battery in action. German minenwerfer dealt with.	
	6th		4 x 50, y50 & 21 Batteries attached since 20/2/17 Bn to rejoin their Divisions. Premature explosion in Y48 Battery (Spelt charge) causing five shell shock casualties.	
	8		Y48 Battery wire cutting in preparation for raid on night of 8/9	
	10th to 16th		X Y Z Batteries in action wire cutting. Weather conditions bad. Snow, rain & high winds.	
	17th		German evacuation of PERONNE lines.	
	19, 20		Mortars withdrawn from lines & brought back to TRN on HERBECOURT - CAPPY ROAD	
	21.		Two 9.45" mortars sent to Trailly	
	22 to 31		Battery	

D.S. Stephen Capt
D.T.M.O

Original. Confidential.

WB/13

War Diary

of

48th Div. Arty. Trench Mortar Batteries

April 1917.

Volume 4. Part 2.

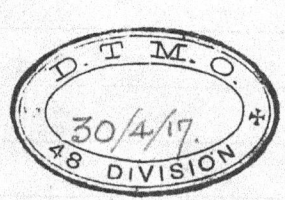

A.E.Hopkins
Capt RFA

48 TRENCH MORTAR BATTERIES R.A.

WAR DIARY or INTELLIGENCE SUMMARY.

Army Form C. 2118.

Place	Date	Hour	Summary of Events and Information	Remarks and references to Appendices
In the Field	April 1-9		Batteries at CAPPY. Working party sent forward to TINCOURT for work on craters etc. Remainder at CAPPY engaged on salvage work.	
	10th		Batteries moved to PÉRONNE	
	11-30		Parties engaged at PÉRONNE in clearing HOTEL DE VILLE of Debris. Forward party at TINCOURT employed in repairing roads, building huts, wiring in battery positions etc.	
	22-29		2/Lt SPENCER and party engaged in building camouflage tank for use in impending offensive operations.	

Watkins Capt RFA

Vol 14

Confidential

War Diary
of
48th Divisional Artillery Trench Mortar Batteries

May 1917

Volume IV / Part II

Army Form C. 2118.

48 TRENCH MORTAR BATTERIES WAR DIARY or R.A INTELLIGENCE SUMMARY.

Instructions regarding War Diaries and Intelligence Summaries are contained in F.S. Regs. Part II. and the Staff Manual respectively. Title pages will be prepared in manuscript.

Place	Date	Hour	Summary of Events and Information	Remarks and references to Appendices
PERONNE	May 1st to 6th		Batteries drilling, & supplying working parties for R.A. H'Qrs at TINCOURT. Lt SPENCER and party building camouflage	
	7th		TANK in accordance with 4th Army instructions. Batteries moved to TREMONT near AMIENS	
TREMONT	8th to 15th		Batteries in training. Marching drill, gun drill, lectures, & shooting on range.	
	16th		Batteries rejoined Division at LE TRANSLOY.	
LETRANSLOY	17th to 19th		Batteries in billets at LE TRANSLOY & finding working parties for D.A.C.	
BEAUMETZ-LES-CAMBRAI	20th to 31st		Batteries improving emplacements in defensive line, taken over from 1st ANZAC DIV, and constructing new emplacements in front defensive line.	

O.W. Williams Capt.

Original.

Confidential.

War Diary

of

48th Divisional Artillery Trench Mortar Batteries

JUNE 1917

Volume V. Part 1.

.... CAPT.
D.T.M.O. 48 Div.

[Stamp: D.T.M.O. 30-6-17 48 DIVISION]

48th Divisional Artillery Trench Mortar Batteries

WAR DIARY

INTELLIGENCE SUMMARY

Army Form C. 2118.

Hour, Date, Place	Summary of Events and Information	Remarks and references to Appendices
BEAUMETZ-LES-CAMBRAI		
June 1st — 6th	Batteries constructing emplacements. Heavy in offensive position before HAVRINCOURT, medium in HERMIES – DOIGNIES – LOUVERVAL defensive line.	
7th	Heavy Battery firing	
8th — 16th	Medium Batteries preparing offensive positions in forward posts & retaliatory purposes. Heavy Battery building emplacement for second gun.	
17th	Heavy Battery in action with both guns. Twenty six rounds fired with satisfactory results.	
18th — 21st	X + Y medium Batteries in action nightly to assist Infantry. Heavy Battery improving emplacements.	
22nd	Heavy Battery in action	
BEUGNY 23rd	Handed over to D.T.M.O 1st ANZAC Div & Batteries moved to CRUCIFIX CAMP Area "J" unemployed & sent to BEUGNY	
MAMETZ 24th	Batteries moved to [?] in working parties. 18th & 4th [?] Divl.

48th Divisional Artillery — Trench Mortar Batteries

Army Form C. 2118.

WAR DIARY
or
INTELLIGENCE SUMMARY
(Erase heading not required.)

Instructions regarding War Diaries and Intelligence Summaries are contained in F.S. Regs., Part II and the Staff Manual respectively. Title pages will be prepared in manuscript.

Place	Date	Hour	Summary of Events and Information	Remarks and references to Appendices
	1-7-17 to 4-7-17		Batteries at BOTTOM WOOD Camp. Fatigue parties of 30 N.C.O's and men supplied daily to D.A.C. Remainder on training parades and inoculation. Z Battery returned from 5th Army T.M. School on the 4th.	
	5 & 6-7-17		Batteries moved to "O" Camp, POPERINGHE.	
	7-7-17 to 10-7-17		Y Battery constructing gun emplacements in the line, remainder camp duties and night fatigues (20 O.R's) for R.E.	
	11 & 12-7-17		Camp fatigues, 18 pdr G.F. drill and work on emplacements	
	12 & 13 M 7-17		X Battery digging emplacement for 6" NEWTON T.M.	
	13-7-17		Batteries moved to 'E' Camp.	
	15-7-17		Batteries moved to bivouac in neighbourhood of VLAMERTINGHE.	
	16 to 20-7-17		X and Z Batteries preparing 2" emplacements, getting up guns, ammunition &c. On the 20th X Battery commenced wire cutting with 6" NEWTON T.M.	
	21-7-17		Y Battery registered with 2" T.M's	
	22 to 25-7-17		Wire cutting by X and Y Batteries, also 6" NEWTON T.M's and 2" T.M's.	
	26-7-17		Two 2" T.M positions taken over from 39th Division by X Battery. Y Battery continued wire cutting.	

Original.   Confidential.

War Diary

of

48th Divisional Artillery Trench Mortar Batteries

July 1917

Volume 5. Part 2.

                    .... Capt.
                         D.T.M.O. 48 Div.

Army Form C. 2118.

WAR DIARY
or
INTELLIGENCE SUMMARY.
(Erase heading not required.)

Place	Date	Hour	Summary of Events and Information	Remarks and references to Appendices
	27-7-17		X Battery fired with 2" T.M⁵ and disposed of several parties of hostile Infantry in the enemy first and second lines.	
	28 & 29-7-17		X and Y Batteries completed wire cutting with 2"T.M.	
	7 & 29-7-17		V Battery, having no guns in action supplied many parties for carrying 6" and 2" ammunition.	

.... Capt.
D.T.M.O. 48 Div.

WAR DIARY
48th Trench Mortar Battery R.A.
INTELLIGENCE SUMMARY

Army Form C. 2118.

August 1917

Place	Date	Hour	Summary of Events and Information	Remarks and references to Appendices
VLAMERTINGHE	August 1st to 3rd		All Batteries withdrawing guns & stores from trenches; inspecting, & cleaning guns and stores.	
	4 to 6		X48 Battery completing maintenance of guns and stores from trenches - V48 and Z48 supplying 40 N.C.Os. men to relieve gun detachments of 241st Brigade R.F.A. Remainder of personnel on 6" Newton T.M. instruction and Camp fatigues.	
	8 to 11		1 Officer, 30 N.C.Os men preparing gun emplacements for 186th Brigade R.F.A. 1 Officer & 40 N.C.Os men attached to 241st Brigade R.F.A. Remainder gun drill, inspection & Camp fatigues.	
	12 to 27		Working parties of from 50 to 100 N.C.Os men & 1 Officer found daily for work at 39th Divisional Ammunition Dump VLAMERTINGHE. Engines thereon were worked by each Battery in turns. Emplacements improved, a gun park laid out & guns mounted thereon, & gun lorries etc carried on. V48 Battery fired over 4 9.45" T.M.	
	28		40 N.C.Os men supplied to work for 241st Brigade R.F.A. carrying ammunition. Remainder of personnel employed on improving the Camp, gun drill & motor inspections.	
	29 to 31		1 Officer 30 N.C.Os men supplied to R.A.M.C. as stretcher bearers. 30 N.C.Os men attached to 241st Brigade R.F.A. for work at gun emplacements.	

[Signature] Capt.
D.T.M.O. 48 Div.

Confidential.   Original.

48th Trench Mortar Batteries. R.A

War Diary.

August 1917.

Volume V Part III

[signature] CAPT.
D.T.M.O. 48 Div.

Army Form C. 2118.

WAR DIARY
or
INTELLIGENCE SUMMARY.
(Erase heading not required.)

48th Division Rauol Krokan Ha. Mons

Place	Date	Hour	Summary of Events and Information	Remarks and references to Appendices
Ha. Leo E.	1st–8th	2.0.	All Batteries: Gun Drill on 2", 6" & 9.45" Howitzers & 17 pm German Leo Runs, Camp improvements & fatigues. daily parades. officers having anti gas class &c.	
	9th, 10th		2 Officers & 2 O.R. detailed for work with 131st Army Brigade R.F.A. Riding for 6" Hows. reminders.	
	11th–15th		Digging positions for 6" Howitzers at MON DU HIBOU. Parades for emplacement course & camp fatigues.	
	16th	12th	2nd & 9.45" Howitzers shoot II Rao 572 & 508 Harassed area 16.508. Division	
			6" Howitzers carried to position at MIM DU HIBOU & put in action.	
	17th, 19th		Carrying ammunition for 6" Howitzers. 2nd 9.45" R.K.I. 4 & 2" Howitzers returned to D.A.R.O.	
	20th		Lent on many fatigues, some for 6" Howitzer during infantry attacks	
	21st		Parades for drill, camp improvements, fatigues &c.	
	22nd, 23rd		Bursting 6" Howitzer and 2 team.	
	6th–27th		20 O.R. attached to 240th Bde. Brigades R.F.A.	
	2nd, 25th		1 Officer & 20 O.R. carrying Ammunition for 58 Divisions Leapd. Krotan Balloons	
	28th		Moved new Camp & 2, 6" Howitzers to 18th Division Rauol Krotan Balloons	
			Batteries remained to NOORDPEENE area	
	29th, 30th		Parades for inspections & training.	

W. D. Harris Capt.

D.T.M.O. 48 Div.

Confidential. _Original._

48th Trench Mortar Batteries, R.A.

War Diary

September 1917.

Volume VI Part I.

[signature]
Lieut.
D.T.M.O. 48 Div.

Army Form C. 2118.

WAR DIARY
or
INTELLIGENCE SUMMARY.
(Erase heading not required.)

48th Trench Mortar Battery, R.A.   October 1917.

Instructions regarding War Diaries and Intelligence Summaries are contained in F. S. Regs., Part II. and the Staff Manual respectively. Title pages will be prepared in manuscript.

Place	Date	Hour	Summary of Events and Information	Remarks and references to Appendices
In the field	1st-4th		Battery at NOORDPEENE. Parades for training & temperature laying.	
	5.		Battery arrived from NOORDPEENE to WINIZEELE	
	6.		Battery moved from WINIZEELE to FLAMERTINGE	
	7-13		All personnel employed at Ammunition Dump on MOAT FARM MOLENE	
			GUN SIDING, VANDOUER. and MILL COTT.	
	14.		Battery moved to ECKE	
	15.		" " to MORBECQUE	
	16.		" " to VENDIN-LEZ-BETHUNE	
	17.		" " to ABLAIN-ST.-NAZAIRE.	
	18,19		In camp. Parades to view the line. Grey 9 in Mortar also used by	
			OAP from 2° Canadian Division.	
	20,21		Parades, and Parades, and 6" Newton Mortar fire from forward line.	
	22		Battery moved to LA TARGETTE. Maj B. Johnsons took over	
			forward parades	
	23-31		Cont on new position	
	26.		2/Lt NEWTON attended hospital DADOS	
			2/Lt BARRON attended hospital. Course at 1st Army School of Mortar	
	30.		2/Lt BARRON to O.R. 1/5 Bn. 2° D.L.I. 15 Bn 2° Q.R. 1/5 Bn to	
			course to 1st Army Mortar School	

D.J. Hamm CAPT.
D.T.M.O. 48 DIV.

Original.   Confidential.

War Diary

of

48th Trench Mortar Batteries R.A.

October 1917.

Volume VI   Part II

D. F. Harris
.... CAPT.
D.T.M.O. 48 DIV.

www.ingramcontent.com/pod-product-compliance
Lightning Source LLC
Chambersburg PA
CBHW081247170426
43191CB00037B/2070